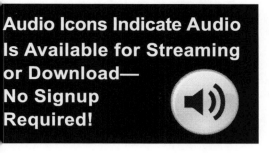

Audio Icons Indicate Audio Is Available for Streaming or Download— No Signup Required!

BIG-N...
Eas...
Kids & Adult Beginners
BY SCOTT CURRIER

GW00676322

ISBN: 9798441809658

HOW TO GET THE AUDIO

The audio files for this book are available for free as downloads or streaming on *troynelsonmusic.com*.

We are available to help you with your audio downloads and any other questions you may have. Simply email *help@troynelsonmusic.com*.

See below for the recommended ways to listen to the audio:

Download Audio Files (Zipped)	Stream Audio Files

Download Audio Files (Zipped)

Recommended for COMPUTERS on WiFi

A ZIP file will automatically download to the default "downloads" folder on your computer

Recommended: download to a desktop/laptop computer *first*, then transfer to a tablet or cell phone

Phones & tablets may need an "unzipping" app such as iZip, Unrar or Winzip

Download on WiFi for faster download speeds

• Recommended for CELL PHONES & TABLETS

• Bookmark this page

• Simply tap the PLAY button on the track you want to listen to

• Files also available for streaming or download at *soundcloud.com/troynelsonbooks*

To download the companion audio files for this book, visit: troynelsonmusic.com/audio-downloads/

INTRODUCTION

Welcome to *Big-Note Bach*! This collection of timeless classical themes is designed to help beginning pianists of all ages learn quickly and easily. What differentiates this book from other piano songbooks? Glad you asked. The most notable differences are:

- **Staff Size:** The arrangements are enlarged so the music is easier to read.

- **Note Names:** Letter names are shown inside each note.

- **Fingerings:** Fingerings are provided for every note.

- **The Melody:** The right-hand melody has been simplified while staying as true as possible to the original composition. The melody can be played solo or performed with the simplified left-hand accompaniment. It's your choice.

- **Key Signatures:** Key signatures are included but accidentals (sharps, flats, and naturals) have been provided in the arrangements for ease of use. Some pieces have been arranged in keys that are different from the original compositions to make them easier to play. Bach's "Minuet in G," for example, was originally composed in the key of G major, but the arrangement in this book is in the key of C major.

- **Audio Tracks:** Two tempos are available with the practice tracks, one at the given tempo and one slower version. Some of the written tempos are slower than what the composer intended in order to make the music easier to play.

THE BASICS

Some basic information on music theory and music symbols are covered on the following pages so even the absolute beginner can play the arrangements.

FINGER NUMBERS

To help you know which fingers play which notes, each finger is assigned a number. Proper finger placement is very important when playing the piano, as it helps with technical efficiency and muscle memory.

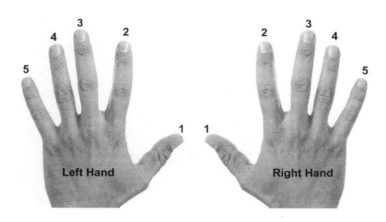

FINGERING

Fingering is a fundamental component of piano technique and cannot be understated. All too often, I've worked with students who do not pay close attention to the fingering or disregard it all together—it's almost as if fingerings are perceived as training wheels that can eventually be taken off. Any competent pianist will tell you that is not the case at all. In fact, the more complicated the piece of music, the more important the fingering becomes.

Sometimes a certain fingering feels awkward, but with practice becomes more comfortable. Have patience with the process. Remember, learning a piece of music involves muscle memory that is developed through consistent repetition. When fingering is inconsistent and constantly changing, muscle memory is nearly impossible to develop, and inconsistent fingering will *always* be an obstacle to mastering a song and playing it with ease.

While fingering is of utmost importance, the fingerings given in this book—or most any book, for that matter—is ultimately a guide, seeing that hands, fingers, and fine motor skills vary from person to person. For the purposes of this book, however, I strongly encouraged you to use the fingerings given as a starting point.

THE MUSIC ALPHABET, TREBLE CLEF & BASS CLEF

The letters of the *music alphabet* are:

A B C D E F G

They are assigned to notes on a *staff*, which consists of five lines and four spaces. The staff is accompanied by a *clef*, which is used to indicate which notes are represented by the lines and spaces. Many instruments utilize just one clef of music—typically either a *treble clef* or *bass clef*. The piano, however, reads *both* clefs at the same time. Treble clef is usually associated with the right hand, while the bass clef is usually associated with the left hand.

Let's see what the line and space notes look like on the staff for each clef:

TREBLE CLEF LINE NOTES

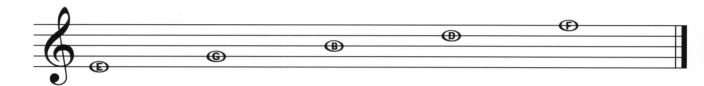

While the letter names of the notes are given throughout this book, memorizing them is beneficial. In addition to repetition, a helpful tip for memorizing the notes is to create a mnemonic device, whereby each word begins with the letter name of the note on the staff. For example, the treble clef line notes would use the following sentence:

<u>E</u>very <u>G</u>ood <u>B</u>oy <u>D</u>oes <u>F</u>ine

TREBLE CLEF SPACE NOTES

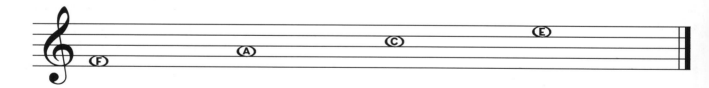

Rather than create a phrase, the treble clef space notes simply spell a word:

F A C E

BASS CLEF LINE NOTES

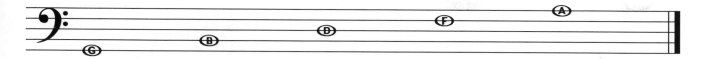

The phrase associated with the bass clef line notes is:

Good Boys Do Fine Always

BASS CLEF SPACE NOTES

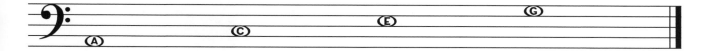

The phrase associated with the bass clef space notes is:

All Cows Eat Grass

Feel free to create your own mnemonic device. Have fun with it!

THE PIANO KEYBOARD

As shown in the diagram below, each of the white keys is assigned a letter of the musical alphabet. The black keys are sharps or flats of the same letters. Simply put, sharps go up and flats go down.

Also, take notice of how the black keys are arranged in groups of 2 and 3—this will help you to memorize where the notes are located on the piano. For example, **C** is always the first white key to the left of the group of 2 black keys, and **F** is always the first white key to the left of the group of 3 black keys.

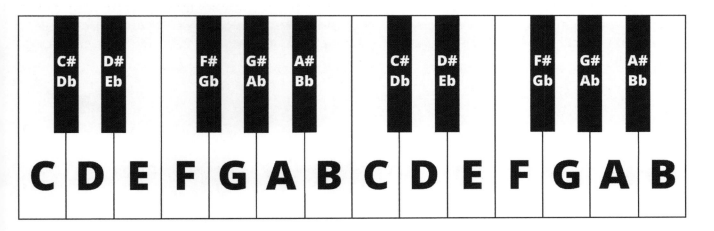

The following diagram illustrates the treble clef notes and where they're located on the piano keyboard:

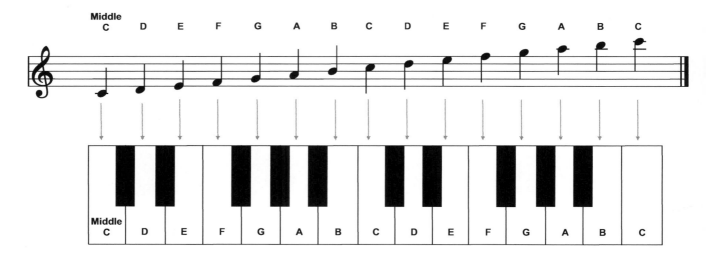

This next diagram illustrates the bass clef notes and where they're located on the piano keyboard:

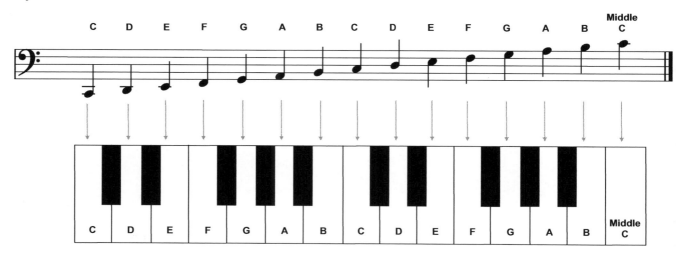

MUSICAL SYMBOLS

In this section, you'll find several music symbols that are foundational to learning piano. Eventually, recognizing these symbols will become second nature, so don't worry about having them memorized right away; instead, feel free to refer to this section as you progress through the book.

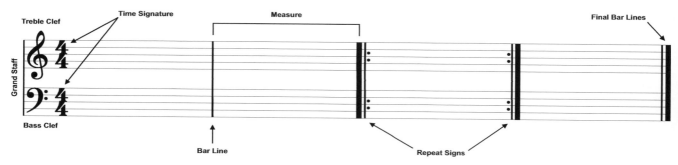

Grand Staff

A combination of the treble clef and bass clef. The grand staff is used to notate piano music.

Time Signature

The *time signature* consists of two numbers. For the purposes of this book, we'll focus on the top number, which indicates how many beats are in each measure.

Four Beats

$$\frac{4}{4}$$

Three Beats

$$\frac{3}{4}$$

Bar Line

A *bar line* is a vertical black line that divides the staff into measures. A *double bar line* indicates the end of a section or passage of music. A *final bar line* (where one line is thick, and the other is thin) is found at the end of a piece of music and signifies the end of the song.

Measure

A *measure*, or *bar*, is used to visually organize the music. Each measure has a certain length (i.e., number of beats) as defined by the *time signature*.

Repeat Signs

In order to save space and help make the music look more organized on the page, repeat signs can be used when the same section of music is to be played again. The *end repeat sign* instructs the musician to go back to the *start repeat sign* and repeat that section of music. Sometimes, repeats will have different endings, which are denoted by numbers above the staff.

Accidentals (Sharps, Flats & Naturals)

Collectively, *sharps, flats* and *naturals* are called *accidentals*. A *sharp sign* raises a note by a half step, or the distance of one key on the piano. A *flat sign* lowers a note by a half step. In most cases, sharps and flats are played on the black keys. A *natural sign* cancels a sharp or flat.

Sharp Sign   **Flat Sign**   **Natural Sign**

♯   ♭   ♮

AIR ON THE G STRING 🔊

J.S. BACH

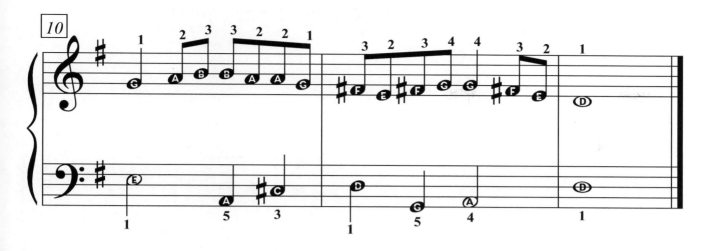

ARABESQUE

FRIEDRICH BURGMÜLLER

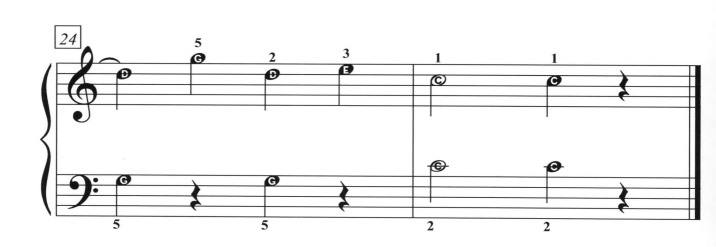

BRAHMS LULLABY

JOHANNES BRAHMS

CANON IN D

hands
together

CARNIVAL OF VENICE

NICCOLO PAGANINI

FINLANDIA 🔊

JEAN SIBELIUS

♩ = 100

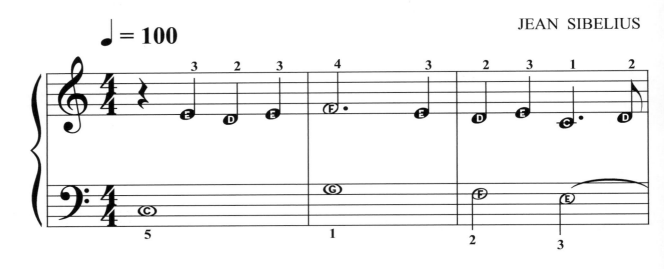

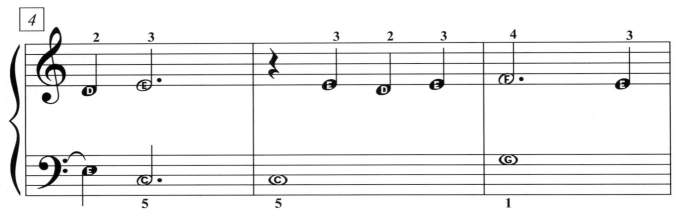

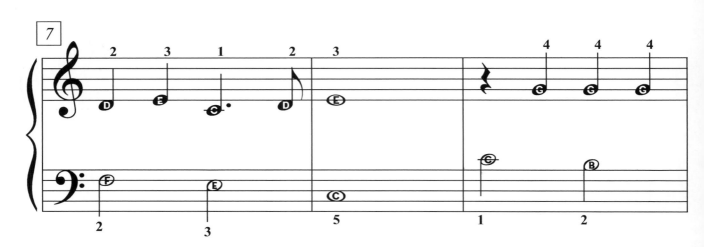

FUNERAL MARCH

FREDERICK CHOPIN

*continue L.H. fingering throughout

FÜR ELISE

LUDWIG VAN BEETHOVEN

29

IN THE HALL OF THE MOUNTAIN KING

EDVARD GRIEG

JESU, JOY OF MAN'S DESIRING

J.S. BACH

MELODY

ROBERT SCHUMANN

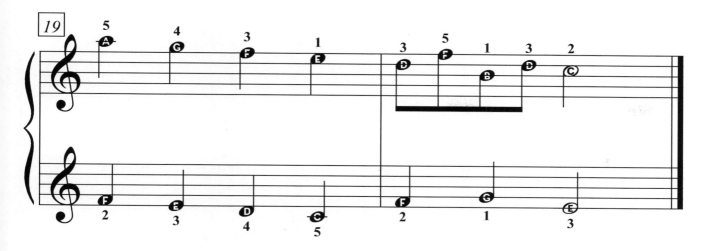

MINUET IN G

J.S. BACH

MINUET IN G

LUDWIG VAN BEETHOVEN

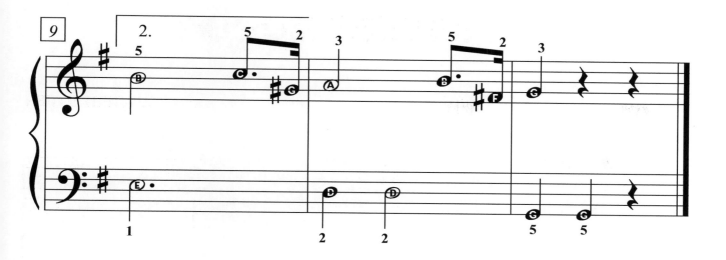

MORNING MOOD

EDVARD GRIEG

NEW WORLD SYMPHONY

ANTONIN DVORAK

ODE TO JOY

LUDWIG VAN BEETHOVEN

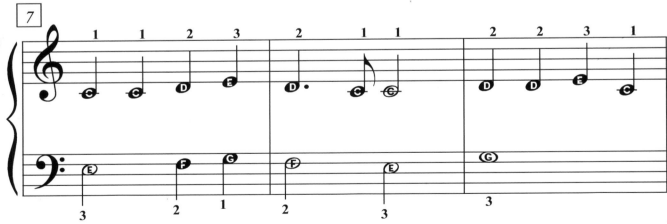

49

RONDO ALLA TURCA

WOLFGANG AMADEUS MOZART

SONATA IN C MAJOR 🔊

WOLFGANG AMADEUS MOZART

SPRING

ANTONIO VIVALDI

SPRING SONG

FELIX MENDELSSOHN

THE BLUE DANUBE

JOHANN STRAUSS

THE WILD HORSEMAN 🔊

ROBERT SCHUMANN

THEME FROM "SWAN LAKE"

PYOTR ILYICH TCHAIKOVSKY

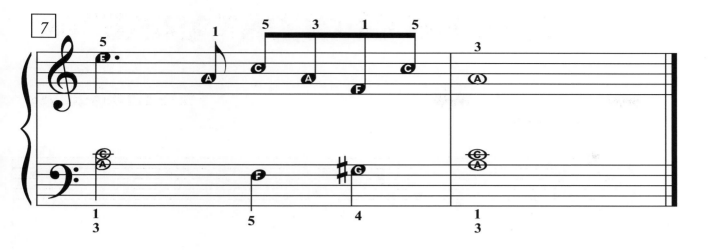

TRUMPET VOLUNTARY

JEREMIAH CLARKE

TURKISH MARCH 🔊

LUDWIG VAN BEETHOVEN

73

WEDDING MARCH 🔊

FELIX MENDELSSOHN

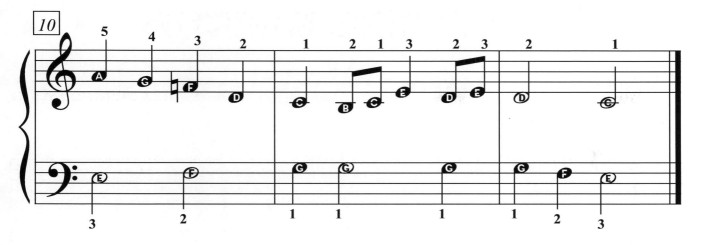

WILLIAM TELL OVERTURE

GIOACHINO ROSSINI

ABOUT THE AUTHOR

Scott Currier has authored and arranged best-selling books such as *16 Easy Christmas Songs for Solo Piano* and *16 Easy Hymns for Solo Piano, Volume 1*. Scott has over four decades of piano experience. He began studying the piano at the early age of 4, when he began to exhibit a natural ability on the instrument. As a classically trained pianist, he developed technical expertise, musicality, and creativity, which prepared him for his studies in jazz and other music genres.

Scott attended the University of Wisconsin–Eau Claire on a full scholarship, earning a degree in Classical Piano. While studying in Eau Claire, he had the opportunity to play with one of the country's top-ranked collegiate jazz ensembles, as well as recording several CDs, including the Grammy-nominated album *Harpoon*. Scott has taught privately for 25 years and continues to freelance extensively across the country as a professional pianist, author, composer, and studio musician due to his expertise in a wide variety of styles.

Printed in Great Britain
by Amazon